TURNERESQUE

TURNER

Burning Deck, Providence 2003

Elizabeth Willis

ESQUE

Burning Deck is the literature program of Anyart: Contemporary
Arts Center, a tax exempt (501C3), non-profit corporation.

ISBN 1-886224-62-5 original paperback
ISBN 1-886224-63-3 original paperback, 50 signed copies

Grateful acknowledgment is made to the editors of the publications
in which these poems first appeared: *American Poetry Review*, *Arshile*,
Aufgabe, *The Baffler*, *Chicago Review*, *Conjunctions*, *Five Fingers Review*,
The Germ, *Hambone*, *How2*, *Mirage*, *New American Writing*, *Quarry West*,
Review of the Cambridge Conference in Contemporary Poetry, and *Shiny*.
"Book of Matthew" was published in *Blood and Tears: A Matthew Shepard
Anthology*. "A Woman's Face" was published in *The Blind See Only
This World: An Anthology for John Wieners*. "Elegy" was published as
a limited edition chapbook by Oasis Press (Portland, ME) in 2000.

CONTENTS

2 SONNET

3 TURNERESQUE

4 ELEGY

5 DRIVE

TURNERESQUE

AUTOGRAPHEME

A thought on the lip
of little sand island

An easy messenger
who forgot where to go

I came to laugh
in a dirty garden

A thwarted pauselessness
considering pearls

I was fluent in salamander

Everything wrote itself onto skin
with a tangled blowing

An opal eye looking down
on an errant package

A sky wrung of tint

What is the meaning
of this minor error?

The reflecting pool
no one could read

A beach fire snagged me
with its bright emergent eye

My colony sought revolt
in every yard

The present was a relic
of a past I was older than

Taking its language, I became an abridgement
of whatever I contained

A social imperative of silky fears

I wanted air
I wanted the balloon

Darkness flaked down like bottle glass
invented by a poor oily sea

A house made of soup

Others formed an invisible order
felt in every part

The male of the species was
louder than the female

Females made the mush
a sound of offstage sweeping

Boys played a game of torment
and sleepy forgiveness

while girls read their books on the rocks
containers of a solar plot

Little bird, fox on a string

A caravan of foreign number
staging death

So?

A smudge against the smallest dress
buried creature, of sly erasures

in the storied night, long *e*
cricketing awake, asleep

MODERN PAINTERS

THE TREE OF PERSONAL EFFORT

after Charles Rennie Mackintosh

The lost highway of ornament fades into origin. Shipwrecks
return like magnets to their builders. In the tree of personal
effort, a balloon is lodged or branches are basketed. What
did we think we dared to sail away from, an unread book, an
aspirin? My body knew I was anchored to earth with flesh.
Build a bigger bellows if you want to rise above your life. So
sighs the pilot's cloud of word. To imply or intone the whole
possibility of human sun. The rose rose unknit with spring.
A dragonfly in your hand for luck.

CATALOGUE RAISONNÉ

after Richard Dadd

A face cut by air
A tangle of feet nearly touching
The eye of a horse and the eye of man
The plane of foreground and background is equal
Stirrups divide assailing and assailed
The grass full of writing
A victim's head contains a letter
the color of water
"Induce" across her hand
beneath her gown
A pillar to support nothing
Two indistinct heads beneath two clear ones
The portion of a foot and spur
One book, one boat
skewed and flattened
What could have been a bear is a tawny cove
What could have been my head is a bunch of windlessness
Two stable surfaces are latched

the door open, or shutting
A tale "interrupted" by its horned start
A change in tone where the fabric is torn

VAN TROMP, GOING ABOUT TO PLEASE HIS MASTERS, SHIPS A SEA, GETTING A GOOD WETTING

after J. M. W. Turner

Constancy scribbles itself out in waves: a revisionary litter of brown light. Fleety with anchor and going abroad, a fulcrum pulls to left of center. A slap in the face of a sail. A device spies down a-swing in salt & gunpowder, an amber passage. Horizons cast their calm tunes. It doesn't take a traitor to overturn a boat. It wouldn't take such amber to blue up the sky. A heavy craft in wordy water, taking on a master. Van Tromp at the prow, asunder surrounded, clothes himself and sets the sail to follow out his inner course. What is his fiction to the boot of manacles, what is I to the future of pain, of boy, of boat life. Afield and legion. The opposite of grass.

THE HEART OF ANOTHER IS A DARK FOREST

after Ford Madox Ford

Believing in my velvet way, I feel the urn to fall dearly.
An ancient light crushing the heavy breath of Man. A
siege or shadow to follow. I am but a child on a carpet,
a democrat called to account for my thoughts. What
more can I hope for than to one day be the subject of a
really good paragraph in a great man's book? Rossetti
"the great man," and everything else is woman. She of
the elaborate mind, who elevates the evening with a
subtle tart. A crystal palace for baking.

LITTLE JOURNEYS

to lovers' houses, a womanly
counterpoint, wall
of revels, plastic love,
a psychic wit, enter Eleanor
Of watery religion, never
stammering, not a few
in dear necessity, virtue suffices:
Polidori to Siddall
Speaking Emerson, not
of Emerson, plainly
the opposite of Dickens
Her floors observe
the hardness of a letter
a pagan sheen
of worthless richness
Within a house
of molten hair
a lover's cloud
'perhaps too late'
nursed to life
but a bauble

overlooking Florence
a July afternoon
utterly perishing
a gaze at the vulgar
a brilliant taker
arrayed in poppies

THE YOUNG BLAKE

sleeps into heaven with his lamps on, finishing explanatory negotiations for a while. *Desert the enemy*. Star formations, sandstone understanding, rock time in general, whatever. Latching onto ecstasy, words that change on waking, clover as a syrup of spring mind. Working off a deficit of sleep or cash, you know who your friends are. Singled out in traffic, lurching into light, having lunch. You're a little one with sand in your eyes, with green on your horn, with milk on your chin. With flowering ears and hearsay.

THREE APPLES, TWO CHESTNUTS, BOWL, AND SILVER GOBLET; OR, THE SILVER GOBLET

after Chardin; for Lisa

As in the darkly open science of the foreground, sheepishly at rest as upon air; the rest we stand in. We stand in for the chestnuts, a type of their magnetism, reflecting on the room; or upon the average darkness, aristocratic brown, with hunted things; we come to rest among them. The painted room, locked in a type of kindness. We reflect upon this lovely habit of this hare with whom we are, in the habit of this picture, getting caught. To hide the virtues of a boundless leaping, we regard reflection in the chestnut. As if the painter drew himself as Death into the still life; as of a sculptural stillness, commas in the dark. A figure of ourselves reflected or a type of picture resting; sheepishly as air, locked in a form of capture.

AFTER BAUDELAIRE

Lost in a room of hermetic fireplaces, locked with the key of sage reflection, you want a fire to singe your skin, a match to play with, but not here, rescued from pleasure by poetry, raining away. Did Coleridge dream of gum disease or was he too absorbed in snuff? We all absorb the surface culture. It breathes us in, sneezing us out every two hundred years. What is happiness? A breeze to sweet-talk drunkenness, a song inking up the night. Or the poem scratching its ring against the roof, stalled out in its own country, where they like you for the perp. Why risk warmth? The embassy is burning. You'll have to make it up to them or erase your way out.

CONSTABLE'S DAY OFF

Loving the human bird—
the bright converse
of yellow-flowered grasses—
why aren't we lying
in miles of weedy clover?
The bright boat, tumbling through it
the blue of it—Or,
taking the kid out of the picture
(what you loved to see)
a girl who talks to birds—Don't go
Let's delay or—like Shakespeare—"fly"
all disappointment
in the green and untidy
molecular air

ARTHUR IN EGYPT

Where do you go after a season in Denver, walking through Africa in shoes of sand. My name was a green flash on the glassy horizon. My pen leaked until there was nothing else to say. When my feet were gone I rowed ashore, beached on the word, *pure*. What happens once can never come again, even in a dream. So I moved on, or it passed through.

2

SONNET

To live in someone
else's music (the musician
not the composer is free)
a divine contention
like the damp carpet
of liquored olivia trees
(something my favorite you
would say) finding
in a hollow day
a winter keeper
a paper woman
caught in the torrent
not quite falling

Carrying an atmosphere
beaten out like sound
a still life of amnesty
on the little lane
Trees are safely tucked
below the wires
a darkness carried
out of childhood
other kindnesses
"I looked"
and fell to

Unable to hire oneself
for labor or to know
the green, braided thing
someone sees
inside you

Forgetting your grasp
or "words"
in a paper understanding
a paper flap of happy self
Your dream above your head
like comic weather

The teacher's love
of someone's children
a flash of light
in white air

So loving love
we lack science
and in ourselves
touch up the little
teacher's picture

Thinking through
a desperate wedge
of indivisible ink
we fall in filaments
an uncontrolled breeze
nutsy, bottled
forged & forgot
Crawling (not climbing) down
netted, I bet

As proud & difficult as Greek
a vigil (or Virgil)
kept bright
waiting to happen
Your father walking
toward your mother
as you briefly look away
then follow like a nonsense syllable
Ma. Pa.

Figs of lost thought
rainy differences and non-glides
feverish in girlways
The tenuous escape of a patient
nodding, obstinate
jeweled or pinked
A pilling station
(laughing, molten)
behind a gay exterior
or broad caplet
too tough to swallow

Our daphne dissipates
a young mist
Must she follow
the if/then into ether
A little myth
in the grass
never hurt anyone
or so
they said
"little apple cake"

A fateful history
beginning to clang
To hunt the doe
in a row of air
Things like sage or virtue
A reader desires
to be crushed by sun
I defile books but
I don't drink beer
Bent into a box
I wrastled fair
I & I
to make it new
or rue among the rose

Anyone has half a life
like salt in groggy sunlight
a dreamed acceleration
forgetfully & fully
there: arena's
circumstance
a textile jolt
awaiting debt
asurf in drift
on peels or wheels

Forgetting the tumbled
sheen of home
we calculate a rescue
out of summer
Lovely missions
in early green
A dream of love
dearest curtain
painted just
beyond the face
a trembling show
attending moonlight
the verso alive
against you

Grammar is coral
a gabled light
against the blue
a dark museum
Durable thing

I find you in a string
I find you every-
where I'm writing
on a leaf, a
satire of flesh-
liness   A tree
is pure intent
and mindlessness
as once, the it
was he or she

Without an arch
triumph is a fantasy
of daily warfare
lunging into nightly airs
Iron can't protect
a feeble word, I'm
less confident
than butter   The blind
limits of a ragged
suggestion: to follow
like an Astor, to belong
to dirt, like a question

3

TURNERESQUE

THUNDER ROAD

Fleeing into fretted sun, he has his reasons. Decoyed and hawked, he fights his battles with moon on his curls. His gal's a singer in an Appalachian bob: a negative dreamboat. He exits windows in broad sun. He crushes hats. He's in sync with rain, doubling his odds of being loved. Leaves shadow him on the wide road. He lives in a hollow. He has more than enough green.

A WOMAN'S FACE

Doctors sculpt a monster to disprove everything. Scaling mountains, she forgives herself the climbs of youth. Nothing can stop her dark mouth. She governs boys carelessly. You can't forge her dazzle. She stars all the time. Acts accrue against her inner caning. She lifts and shoots in furs, criming her way to newness, men. She carries herself like a parcel over waterfalls bejeweled in salt. Her breath is honeysuckle in winter. Mourning doves carry her by the shoulders. Shaking curls against her neck, caught in a lie, she mines inwardly for change. Her forehead glows like cream above the Austrian ego. She can read.

CLASH BY NIGHT

A good man's up to his waist in mackerel. Sometimes there are no other fish in the sea. A stormcloud roils over his primitive kitchen. Her eyes are starlight headed for a crash. She wants the part, but not for long. Dancing shows everyone where she comes from. The projectionist is a dark horse, but he's at home there. The pin-up's a bunny in jeans, drinking milk, thinking up babies, a lesson in endurance. The martyr trades her wings for a day at the beach, but who can blame her? You can't reform a lighthouse. The worker knows he's been gulled. His catch is no match for *noir*.

THE UNKNOWN

Moonlight has a human grip. Silver light glints against desire. The impostor is a hero villain. He has our love. Nothing repulses him like the truth. Ingenuity seeks its goal and is trampled. Nothing itches more than vengeance. Scratch. Dexterity files a suit against strength. Strength wins. This is justified. A glitter whip is no match for evil. The girl moves between men like a child tossed in the air. She is always in costume, floating above us like a thumb.

THE WOLFMAN

A man with a cane has made a long trip. He's unstrung, coming home. Trapped, in agony, he heals in moony thickets. He gives away pentagrams. He tiptoes through fog. He's as good natured as Jesus. An errant son with an aversion to pity, he's reluctant to love. He shoots paper ducks but can't hit the canine. In a plaster forest he's riddled by replicas. He needs a shrink. He's bound to the gypsy by a terrible necklace. You can't protect everyone from yourself.

DON'T BOTHER TO KNOCK

Nel's off the farm, watched over by a dutch uncle. She writes herself in semaphor and scars. Her story's on a timid fuse of torment like the girl behind the wall. Pilots are never what they appear, flying over Oregon. Even when they tiptoe she hears the watery crash of slamming doors. She meets a creep half made of memory, but his girl's already got him with a sultry lasso. Nel's looking for an ally. But when the house dick comes to, she's already walking the arena into old rooms. It's a wrap.

ON DANGEROUS GROUND

Jim's a bad one whining down a concrete river slick with night. Another wrong punch and he'll be badgeless. A bloodhound sent to hicksville on a sleeper, he stumbles on a country missile. She feels her way to the smoothest things. She builds an indelible fire. Her brother's heart is an inward tree, but he's got blood on his hands. Love gropes them more than blossoms. Jim's been wrong before, but now he's pinned by the discreteness of her body in the dark. There's no turning back for a cop with snow in his shoes. She leans into his face: the hardness of water. The fluidity of land. The total radiance of faces in a mine. He sinks against her ivy wall. There's no telling where she'll lead.

THE MONSTER

You wake up crashing through an image of yourself. You're a wreck, waiting for your turn under the electric cap. Only the dick-by-mail suspects the truth. He's a fool, playing with shadows. Caliban brings you in from the storm like a zombie savior. The hero walks an electric tightrope. He's a robin in spring jacket. You should have been dancing. Maybe the monster is right: the girl is suddenly beautiful on the table, facing her doom, ready to marry the man who saves her.

TARZAN, THE APE MAN

Cheetah touches the river and cries. Tarzan belongs to vines, as Jane belongs to the wavy boy-man who can call a stampede like a taxi home. He's making darkness safe for the Colony. He's beating a croc across a lake. He's holding her Brancusi head between his hands. He's showing her team a field of ivory, and if she'll grab the elephant's paper ear and ride it home, he'll fan out all his hidden plumage.

THE WILD BUNCH

Men ride toward the cleaners like steam through the train. Everyone's a gentleman in somebody's book. Poor purple monograph bunched up on a mule. By the time they wash up in Mexican water the little bird is just a dirty umbrella, a word game played out beneath the sun, blood on the wire. Somewhere out of town they know they've been salted. They'll machine-walk these limbs into town till the end spells them out in big red drops.

FLIGHT ANGELS

Chick flies too high, testing the stratosphere. Mary's out to save him, but he's got her by the wings. In the middle of a dirt field, she wants the man with a nosebleed. Love is not the only form of blindness. She's like a yellow rose stuck in his hand. He's got the odds of the oldest racehorse in the world, but she won't let him lose. They'll live out their transference with recruited smiles in a world prepared to witness death, in feathers, out of view.

MAYOR OF HELL

Lunch is a stomp of shabby caps and overbites in
Peakstown. A boy so frail he is all nose. You eat in silence
and hold hands across the night. The super is an Irish
sleeper with a whip up his sleeve. But Patsy can top him;
his okay is a rational assault on reform. He's your missing
Pa. He'll teach you how to beat a rap and be American
at once, putting out the fires he starts. He knows how to
love a nurse.

A STOLEN LIFE

Siblings are forever, spinning out fate like an evil twin. Artist & model, the sailor and the tart. She's painted herself into a mirror. When she turns around, it's Pat, living out the logic of her ambiguity, stealing boyfriends for kicks. Sure the guy tumbles, but who can love a cake for more than a night? She'll wait forever, an extravagant island. He's shown her the spume of his special place. She gets loved by accident, the one without frosting. Her sex is deep and refracted. She can hold her own at sea.

KISS ME DEADLY

Christina Rossetti papers London with canary flyers. The next thing she knows, she's falling into headlights, lying in toxic sedge. She's dead all right. She's swallowed the key into the language of America. She's invested in advertising. It's a nuclear secret, a box of smack, and she's its beachhead. She's come from the dead to be remembered, and if she has to kill someone along the way, that's poetry.

It's turneresque in twilight. The word comes at me with its headlights on, so it's revelation and not death. I figure I'm halfway home though I've only started. Nothing is moving but me: I'm a blackbird. The neighbor's in labor, but so am I, pushing against the road. Physics tells us nothing is lost, but I've been copping time from death and can't relent for every job the stars drop on my back.

4

ELEGY

ELEGY

The day I drove

in a driving rain
from realism to impressionism

a moving hillside fooled the town

What does it take
to make a happy ant?

a dropped lozenge
on the damp step

bumping into a friend
in the daily grind

avoiding death

Still you slip away
in a desert hospital

and cannot see to see

Hawthorne's hand
against your hair

the stumbling blue
of windowed air

■

What unknown slippered thing of x is thou
a dirty engine shooting out the star
a decoy aurora'd in fig
I myself
in plain flesh, answer

The soul's a fine thing
less than feathers
free to glitter
in no-light night

a petticoat of sand
the mind's a hinge
a roughly chestnut arsenal
a little box of nothing
an incidental rose

∎

If a dove spoke
lifted into goldleaf

—leaving for home
like a fox through mint

a canned geranium
like what you see is—

would we understand

■

I hobble into sun-gray air
to feel the carbon in my hair

Fins of centuries brushing by

I felt the grass's poem
blown against me
like a fake harp

like the harmony of deluge
before I seen you
subtly from behind
the dewy lumber of my eye

An Ozymandias
permanent as plastic
forever underneath

■

A green sky figured
flickered out against
a life given up to cement

Athena, our hesitant barn owl
regal as a cigar band in rain

Where's the organ an animal forgives with
Where's my "heart" within the cells I cotton to

To flurry and ark the lumber of sky
a boat of white enamel, a step into the yard

like a tin adventure
blown forward in a crowd

■

Threading a life
of levered paradox

snowy patterns of the arch composer

in feathered mud
to lean aground

to leave behind
an almost empty ivy mind

feet that are roots
a piece of string
that is a mountain

a flight of color
disturbed into line

When I was a fish
I didn't have to answer

being in a bush or hand
a face in locomotion

that crashes in between

A FISHER KING

Falling in the alley
or shadow of debt

beauty yields
beyond all earning

A glitter train
against the sun

inventing a bobby
fischer to live through it

Dear comet
dear rook

who couldn't see
the stardom on your body

empires of loneliness
on board

Hand against
the flyaway clock

a lasting silver lid
or gulf you fancied youngly
for a day

Like Turner with his legs
upon the orly grass

thinking treed hills
in tweedy blue

his mothered shadow
a lavender turbine

an ancient wisteria
lugging up groundwater

What you take
onto the surface

above the brow
is fierce emergence

O hero of the leafy mind

you're out of reach
in parabolic lamplight

its burning eye
whatever you wanted

INGRID WASHINAWATOK

Tenderly buttoning its gaze
across an inner lawn
California dreams of nativity
filtering green through fine mesh
A magnolia with hell to pay
turning to beer   A dirty table
aiming for your head
like the lemon punch
of headlines   House wins
Where's Patton when you
need him, making patent leather
boots?   I couldn't reach
nirvana if it reached me first
A nickel never hurt anybody
but a book can get you killed
I'm sure I'll come back
as a spider someone like me
will crush and send to sea
or the ant endlessly
walking my ceiling

looking for the stairs
Whose side are you on?
That of the "girl"
i.d.'d by tattoos
who dared to cross into
the human camp

WITHOUT PITY

To embark sleepily
being everywhere
(radiant)
To fashion oneself
wholly after dogs
to talk oneself out of
a beautiful illness
eschewing affection
and envying lilies
How were the fish eaten
the fire carried
if beauty came
only by restraint
How does a ghost eat?
Even Mary crumbled under piety—
her stone son
Understanding misery
never to desert it

What can be forgiven
of its dangerous body

(not a constant)
To find the branch
of an underground river
while tongues wag out
the weakest things
To escape design
(its "higher calling")
To make or love
anything
To hate the agony
of any human thing

BOOK OF MATTHEW

for Matthew Shepard

Here's a text that's mixed with others
wired into snowcone snow
what you see and what you get
a block from the Union Pacific
against a ten-mile fence of news

My great-uncle was a train man
strictly steam, he never got over
the Twentieth Century

My brother was born in Casper
the wind was a joke
a mean metal syllogism
with nowhere to go

You've been indexed
& written in pencil on bedroom walls
& like Shelley, writ in light
in a mind the size of a coin
conceived as memory
the beginning of sorrows

MY FELLOW AMERICANS

who came to see
a baby in a star
a virgin in a chair
a boy who walks a book
crossing like a gold comet
afloat in painted milk

Preferring an arch to a peak,
a pear to understanding
I think I live
to clink among the clams
forgetting the edge of my twin
Everything eventually falls into
the opposite of water
A ticking landscape pulls down
heaven into atmosphere
It's in our paper plot, our life of flowers
to sun, to sink, to water the planets
pinching tickets, bending the bow
Earthlings of modest parentage
of unsure origin, of orange hair
adrift across Wyoming

in sandals, into bloom
The building will fall
like a little tree
of creaturely Magritte
I haven't forgotten
my boots of Spanish lead or
the khaki nothing
between painted things

Regarding impermanence
we're almost there
Dear Mike & Debbie
in the heat of '82
Don't accept
impermanent cement
an eyelash wish
Regard impermanence
dear Mike & Debbie
Regard the flying boy

5

DRIVE

Not a cathedral but rather a railway or one's private automobile "locates" human concern and effort: the conveyance which contains intrinsically no reference ...

LILIANE & CYRIL WELCH

Trouble fell weeping at the sight of paved-over love. Distinctions that hold branches apart against sky, seeing it through lenses or even the eye if round. The final heat of a negative drifting off the road, inside outside. I fell I snowed I conjured into not. Fixed annoyance, detailed love. Sinkers, undesperate, are always the last donut. And this once pair, a final spelling in figments of polish, of door.

Felt things last longer than seen things, says who, drawing out forks of fire, who walking by, tied for departure, packaged into powder. Fled ecstasy as a response like "brilliant" can mean anything. Everything appears to shine given enough darkness. Crushed into brilliance, the bright ball, dished. Write your poem in the space above, erasing what is beneath it. Paper covers rock. Listen. It's tough, hearts get crushed by metal these days, no matter what.

What last broke against leaf, under leaf-bearing mind?
So little disturbs the sea by comparison. Do you mind?
Finding a reflected mountain is really a shadow, a tree
is beneath its color, the shore a mirage. A real boat in
imaginary water. Yellow fall, green gilled. Trees have the
only real land-legs. Consider our end. The lights are dry
in daylight, up in the dipper, the Hammer, scorpion, the
Hurricane. The kid's fire is hidden, underneath. To crawl
out from under. It's dirt. Don't win. Don't put it out.

Haze horns in with ire for summer. Even bad dreams spill through into morning: waxy cylinders of belted sunlight. We Never Close. A western anthem. In my mother's mouth are many scansions, but earthliness has something wanting in spite of its honey. When I was a bud I hustled sandbags for a quarter. I wore the bell. I sent or sat among daisies. Translate the dollar. Follow that pen. Fall for piffle, yet. I miss the town that born me.

Girl goes home, goes down, a slippery symptom. Boy declines behind haircut, unfair across its table, vast, flat, table, tipping, lost, left, a peach. Free in time and heart before four, they're mediterranean, a listed number. Particular, open, improbable, lichen, long eared, overhead, parallel. I hear the clanging just out of reach, my thought following. Bitten by. Broke. It's too young, the rose that blocks my window. I mean to last.

What you rise out of may not be dirt, but what you breathe must be air. On an indigo chart, we drive without a future, left to wish outside the forward rush of things. Who would not leave the mess for the illumination, the culture for the poem? Believe in inconstancy, a colorist. Forgetting the orangist is only a pomologist, not a painter sent home for lack of design. The night's a plateau. Where would we be in desert night, deserted. Constantinopilized. Oranged.

Valley genes, screening for dust, pump off beauty for a bite. A patinaed stream gutting noon. A town coined with lace. Is it a dove in mourning or homo erectus on a roll to the Genghis Kitchen? Blowing oreward, open-handed, in faulted nature, flushed. An excellent copy, reluctantly boarded. Slightly foxed. Otherwise, fine.

A curtained battle prize of me, not-me, shaken into sweat. A drive-in ecstasy of float, throated. Is disingenuity a glimpse of fabrication, or the lie of nature, satinized, distinct, in linen life? A livid feature of face arranged on plastic, shadowed or ennumbered. An alpine trigger draped in product. The girl missed or missing. The surface of painted water is riddled with oars, a bridge crowned with bullets for thorns.

A fool by nature, daylight beats me up. A trim surrender coughing out lemons. A tear of summer gasoline or an insect chipping away at morning, caught in my ear. Maybe it's not the tool I wanted. Digging my mother for her fortitude, my father for lasting. Everything has a pattern, but that's not all in the little white room, asleep in the drift, the life on paper.

In simple shade an indigent itinerary is lost against the effort to get there. A feel copped then forgotten. An echo afforded from, I couldn't guess. Built, fanatical landscape; unheralded heroic absences. Figured out plainly in numbers or sticking the mind with words. Ticking out like native stuffing, wishing in a wing, exiting right or left; sticking around. I give up the song. It hides. It wants the plum I never had, in a metaphorical garden, forgetting its naked self, no longer nude.

The day left off with a kind of singing "bang." Golden-rod in a small sea-like air, specific and unbroken. I cannot favor hunger or its alternatives. I cannot describe salt. In a parallel universe does anything intersect the confused blossoming blueness of a wall that is not sea, not golden-rod, but the paper fastening of you, standing against it? I favor concrete between our rage and its mirage. Its broken line. Catch the flying saucer but spit out its metal mystery. Adore the big green nothing of the past, the rationing of calm late in the century, like the arches of a brick heart, letting go.

TURNERESQUE *WAS DESIGNED FOR BURNING DECK SEPTEMBER 2002 BY QUEMADURA,*
SET IN MONOTYPE FOURNIER, AKZIDENZ GROTESQUE, AND LINOSCRIPT, AND PRINTED BY
KROMAR PRINTING LTD., CANADA, ON ACID-FREE PAPER. THERE ARE 1000 COPIES, OF
WHICH 50 ARE NUMBERED AND SIGNED.